Dear S

Dear Santa,
Thank you for the skateboard

Dear Santa,
Thank you for the spaceship.

Dear Santa,
Thank you for the kite.

Dear Santa,
Thank you for the watch.

Dear Santa,
Thank you for the bike.

Dear Santa,
Thank you for the kitten.

Dear children,
Thank you for the cookies.